DEDICATION

For my children,
Alyssa, Courtney, Joshua, and Jason,
and our sons-in-law, Luke and Aaron.
Their lives are divinely given gifts.

Keeping Up with Jesus

A
Narrative Devotional Commentary
on Mark

Allan R. Bevere

Energion Publications
Gonzalez, Florida
2023

Copyright © 2023, Allan R. Bevere. All Rights Reserved.

Scripture quotations are from New Revised Standard Version Bible, copyright © 1989 National Council of the Churches of Christ in the United States of America. Used by permission. All rights reserved worldwide.

Cover Design: Henry E. Neufeld

ISBN: 978-1-63199-891-1
eISBN: 978-1-63199-892-8
Library of Congress Control Number: 2023952027

Energion Publications
1241 Conference Rd
Cantonment, Florida 32533

pubs@energion.com
energion.com

Table of Contents

Dedication iii
Introduction vii

Chapter 1 1
Chapter 2 5
Chapter 3 9
Chapter 4 13
Chapter 5 17
Chapter 6 21
Chapter 7 25
Chapter 8 29
Chapter 9 33
Chapter 10 37
Chapter 11 41
Chapter 12 45
Chapter 13 51
Chapter 14 55
Chapter 15 59
Chapter 16:1-8 63
Chapter 16:9-20 67

Introduction

For some years, I have been fascinated with Mark's Gospel. In my younger years, I was more focused on Luke and Matthew. They are longer and fill out stories where Mark is only brief. In fact, it is the continual temptation to neglect the Second Gospel because it is so sparse in comparison. For example, Mark has only two verses on Jesus' temptation in the wilderness while Matthew and Luke go into more detail. Mark has no birth narrative either.

But as I did more study in Mark, I became fascinated by it in large part because of its brevity. In the modern West, we live in a fast-paced world where at times it is difficult to catch our breath and Mark seemed well-suited to that world. In Mark, Jesus is always in a hurry and throughout the Gospel the disciples are continually two steps behind him in their understanding of Jesus, who he is and what he is teaching the crowds. One of Mark's favorite words is "immediately," *euthys* in the Greek. Of the 58 times *euthys* is used in the Gospels and Acts, 41 of those occurrences are in Mark. There's a sense of urgency in Mark that is not felt in the other Gospels. The arrival of Jesus on the scene almost feels like an immediate departure as if the train is leaving the station and one has to run to hop aboard. There is no time to ponder or deliberate. The Kingdom of God has arrived. It is knocking at the door and the decision to answer the door is now or never. Perhaps the faced-paced story of the gospel of Mark offers us counsel on our faced-paced lives in the twenty-first century? The problem may not be so much that we are busy as that we are busy with the wrong things. Mark may assist us in rethinking *how* we are busy.

Writing this kind of commentary on the Gospels is something I have wanted to do for years and starting with Mark was always my intention. In part, it may be because the general consensus is that Mark was the first gospel written, but the sense of urgency in Mark is a reminder of why the Jesus story must be told. To be first seems all the more appropriate.

I refer to this work as a *Narrative Devotional Commentary*. It is devotional in that it assists the reader in their spiritual journey as well as a commentary that retells the story of each gospel in narrative form. It is a commentary, but not in the standard sense. There is little documentation except when necessary. It is to read like a story, a story about the story with each chapter starting with a contemporary connection as a reminder that this story is for us some twenty-one centuries later. Whether this book lives up to that format, the reader must judge.

At the end of each chapter, including this introduction are three questions meant for further reflection. This is to assist the reader in their devotional time. They are also meant to begin a discussion if this work is used in a group Bible study. These are not the only questions to be asked. I hope they will give birth to further questions for consideration.

Questions

1) Have you studied Mark previously? If so, what do you remember?
2) What do you hope to learn from Mark?
3) Are there any particular questions you have as you begin?

Chapter 1

The 1970s sitcom, "All in the Family" centers on the characters of Archie and Edith Bunker. Archie is not the sharpest pencil in the box and his wife Edith often comes off as humorously ditzy, but often has a depth of insight that shows through when needed.

One of the contrasts between the couple is that Archie doesn't have much patience especially when it comes to listening to explanations. He wants people to get to the point—just the facts. The problem for Archie is that Edith can never get straight to the facts. As she explains to Archie what happened, she meanders all over the place. In frustration, Archie makes his typical disgusted face and says to Edith, "Geesh, Edith! Get to the point!"

Archie would have appreciated Mark. He does not waste any time getting to the point. He does not stop to ponder the birth of Jesus as do Matthew and Luke. He does not begin with any lofty and soaring theological introduction like John. Mark starts with the words, "The beginning of the gospel of Jesus Christ the Son of God." With these words he is off and running. There is no time to lose. The time is short; it is time to repent for the Kingdom of God is knocking at the door.

Mark is in a hurry to tell the story. He uses the word "immediately" more than the other three Gospels combined. Mark tells the story of John the Baptist without much detail—only enough to prepare the way for Jesus. He comes to John to be baptized. There is no protest from John that he is unworthy to perform such an act on God's Anointed.

The dove appears, the voice of God speaks, and immediately Jesus is driven into the wilderness to be tempted. He does not move on his own initiative as if he knows his first duty after baptism. The Spirit pushes Jesus into the desert as if he is uncertain of what to do next, or perhaps he knows what needs to be done, but needs that extra divine "push" to face what lay ahead. It is a reminder to us that perhaps even the Son of God needed some prodding to get moving in doing what was necessary

Jesus will, after all, be in a hostile place with the "wild beasts." In the Garden of Eden, Adam and Eve lived in harmony with the animals of the garden. Unlike Adam, Jesus resides in a gardenless desert with wild untamed beasts. Whereas Adam had dominion over the animals and even named them, Jesus must contend with the danger of other creatures made by the Creator of all things. Jesus wrestles with the discontinuity of the world not as it should be. The wolf had not yet lay down with the lamb as the Prophet Isaiah envisioned. When Easter arrives, Jesus, the Second Adam will have conquered the beasts, but for now he will face them on their territory. No wonder the angels come to minister to him.

When Jesus emerges from the wilderness, he is ready to embark on his ministry. He calls his first disciples who follow him in the same immediate fashion in which he was shoved into the desert. Perhaps Jesus' time with beasts in the field prepares him for his first victory over an evil spirit that possesses a man. It is important to note that in Mark's Gospel, the only persons addressing Jesus as "the Son of God" are God the Father (1:11; 9:7), the demons (3:11; 5:7), and the Gentile centurion at the cross (15:39). Everyone else who comes in contact with Jesus during his ministry, including the disciples fail to recognize who he truly is in their midst. The demons will show themselves smarter than many of the religious leaders; for at least the spirits recognize him.

Jesus begins his work by healing; and we begin to get a glimpse of why Mark is in such a hurry to tell the story. Something is now happening in this Jesus that has never happened before. While God has moved throughout history, in this Jesus it appears that God is doing a new work; perhaps it will be a work that will bring God's will to completion. Perhaps God is doing in this Jesus what will be the climatic solution to Israel's plight. Jesus has come not just as another good teacher to point out how to live a good life. He is not one more sage in a long line of wise people. His life is so significant that it has attracted the attention of the powers of darkness. They know something big is afoot in the world as Jesus travels Galilee and Judea, and they don't like what they are witnessing. The demons move to act.

Is it any wonder then that Jesus has to pause for prayer? Without prayer, our Lord will not be able to fulfill the mission for which he came.

Questions

1) Mark's Gospel has a sense of urgency. While busyness is not always a good thing, how do we prioritize the necessary urgencies in our lives?
2) In Mark's Gospel, most people including the disciples do not recognize Jesus for who he is. What are things that keep people from recognizing Jesus today?
3) If prayer was critical for Jesus, it should be critical for his followers. What things can hamper our prayer life?

Chapter 2

Once you've become famous, it is difficult to spend quiet time where people know you. Many people dream of fame, but when some manage to get it, they find it is a blessing and a curse. Lia Beck writes of one famous actor's attempt to avoid the spotlight.

> George Clooney is one of the most famous actors there is, and the fact that you don't hear about him all the time is on purpose. Instead of living in Los Angeles, Clooney, his wife Amal Clooney, and their two children live on secluded properties in England and Italy, out of the spotlight. "Fame can be very dangerous, because you can start to enjoy that part of it," Clooney told Omega's Lifetime magazine in 2012. "And that's not the good part of what I do for a living. The good part is the making of films. The unpleasant part is the fame part, if you're not careful."[1]

Jesus has become famous in Galilee. He does not seek the spotlight, but neither does he avoid it. He has returned to Capernaum, the headquarters for his ministry, and he is teaching to a crowd so large that people are crowded outside the windows of the house, straining to hear and learn from this rabbi's wisdom.

Four friends of a certain paralyzed man carry him on a mat to Jesus in the hope that he will be healed. There are so many gathered around, that the men cannot even get their friend close enough to Jesus to experience his healing touch. Is it possible

---

[1] Lia Beck, "17 Major Celebrities Who Actually Hate the Spotlight," https://bestlifeonline.com/celebrities-who-hate-being-famous/.

to imagine the great disappointment and anxiety this man in need felt as his cure lay not quite within his grasp?

But loyalty and love are a great combination for persistence. In the twenty-first century, these four men would be arrested for the willful destruction of property, but perhaps the needs of a man in bondage to the frailty of the human condition outweigh the need of having a roof.

In healing the man, Jesus does not simply restore his health, but does something that only God can do; he forgives the man his sins. A human being may be able to forgive others the sins that are committed against her, but no one is able to forgive someone else's sins in general. The scribes understand this and protest. Of course, if Jesus were only a man, the scribes' objections would be quite appropriate; but they do not realize who this Jesus is in actuality. The readers of Mark's Gospel are in-the-know about Jesus in a way the characters in the drama are not. The synoptics may not have the emphatic high divine Christology of John, but neither do they lack one. In forgiving the man his sins, Jesus is declaring in no uncertain terms that what was previously available only at the Temple was now available through him. The implications are clear and it angers the religious leaders. If divine forgiveness of sin is now available through this Jesus, then the Temple is no longer unique. In fact, it may now have become obsolete.

With the drama of healing over and the people expressing their amazement, Jesus returns to the task of gathering his twelve disciples who will represent his reconstituted Israel. Levi, a tax collector, one viewed as a traitor by most Israelites for his willingness to collect revenue for a foreign and occupying power, is called by Jesus and immediately he follows.

The invitation to discipleship is given to all, but Jesus seems more interested in extending it to the people who need it the most, and who would never be given one by the "righteous" religious leaders. They may protest that such people are unworthy, and that Jesus implicates himself as one who lacks "righteousness" by keeping company with them. Of course, their logic is quite flawed. Just as a doctor is called into the world of the sick, so Jesus has been called into the world of the sinner. And this Jesus is not only able to do for others physically what trained physicians cannot do, he is able to accomplish for all sinners, tax collectors and Pharisees alike, what no one else in the world can accomplish—bring healing to the entire person.

And what a joyful moment this Jesus brings as the divine walks among women and men. So much so that these new followers of Jesus do not fast, as is the custom for the "righteous." How can one fast at a wedding reception? How can one fast on the day of a holiday celebration? To be sure, there will come a day when those first disciples will fast. By the end of his earthly ministry, Jesus may have indeed completed his work, but much has yet to be fulfilled. The joyful times will overlap with times of suffering.

But can there be doubt that in this Jesus, something new is afoot in the world? The lame walk, sinners are forgiven, and Sabbath is a day for true renewal and rest; a day God made for his beloved humanity, the rules of which are not governed by the fence-minding Pharisees, but by the Lord of the Sabbath and every other day of the week.

Questions

1) Being a celebrity has benefits and pitfalls. What can Jesus' popularity teach us about how to handle celebrity status in a healthy way?
2) Since Jesus is able to forgive sins, Mark is hinting at Jesus' divinity in no uncertain terms? Who is Jesus for you?
3) In calling twelve disciples Jesus is performing a symbolic act of forming a new community, a new people of God. It has been said there are no Lone Ranger Christians. Why is community necessary for discipleship?

Chapter 3

Have you ever felt you were being watched? I have African American friends who testify that often they are under scrutiny when they are in white sections of town, either browsing in a store or walking down the street. Some of them have stated they have been stopped by white police officers for no reason other than to ask them what they are doing in that neighborhood as if they have no right to be there. No one likes to be a suspect.

The religious leaders are suspicious of Jesus. They already consider Jesus to be a Sabbath-breaker and now they watch him as he enters the synagogue to see if he will heal on a day of rest, so that they might accuse him. Never mind the fact that Jesus is about to dramatically change a man's life, never mind that the Sabbath was instituted by God as a day that was to be re-creative. Even though Jesus' miracles are an indication that God is now preparing to institute the final drama of redemption in which all things will be restored, a time in which Sabbath will become, not an interval of twenty-four hours, but an eternal re-created state to be enjoyed by all of creation, those entrusted with the oracles of God cannot stretch their necks far enough to see over the horizon of what God is doing in Jesus. Instead of seeing the miracles of Jesus as individual glimpses, previews, of what is to come, they are fixated on what is, and therefore, in their minds, what must always be. They are so intent on what they want, that the religious leaders conspire with their opponents the Herodians, those persons who support the dynasty that most in Israel consider to be illegitimate. How true it is that often, especially when it comes to politics, the enemy of my enemy is my friend. From this time on, Jesus is a marked man.

Of course, Jesus is not to be deterred. He has a mission to complete and there is no time to waste. He takes a break from his work long enough to appoint his twelve disciples, his reconstituted Israel, who will press on after his earthly mission is completed. What a group he chose! If there was ever a motley crew, this was it—fishermen, a traitorous tax-collector, and a zealot, who made a habit of killing tax-collectors. An expert in personnel today would question Jesus' ability to pull together a winning team; but the work of the Spirit can do what not even a legendary coach can accomplish. God will take these men and in the power of the Spirit, God will change the world.

In choosing this diverse group of men, Jesus was also glimpsing the kind of community he had envisioned for the future. This Body of Christ, as it would later be called, was a community of great diversity centered around the one commitment of following the One who called them. God's newly reconstituted people in Jesus was to be unified, but not uniform. Without the different parts of the Body functioning for the good of the whole, the Body could not effectively fulfill the mission Jesus was calling it to embody as his presence. Of course, such diversity makes unity a challenge as we will see in the Gospels themselves with the disciples at times bickering among themselves. Yet, the dynamics of such unity in diversity will attract many who seek something new and different.

And as the Body, the disciples will need the Holy Spirit, for the message they will proclaim has a jagged edge, that scandalizes even those who desire to be faithful. Even Jesus' family and friends are now beginning to wonder about his sanity. Some claim that he has a demon, but Satan doesn't do the wonderful re-creating deeds that Jesus is accomplishing. Later on, the imprisoned John the Baptist will send his disciples to Jesus asking if he is indeed the promised Messiah. Jesus will appeal to them to tell John what they see and hear. The blind see, the lame walk, and the poor are hearing that the Good News is for them too! If Satan is doing his work through Jesus, he is contributing to his own undoing.

But it is not only the scribes who are questioning allegiances. Jesus raises his own questions as well. He understands that one of the most sacred idolatries can be family, blood-relations. Jesus' words no doubt sting when he says, "Whoever does the will of God is my brother and sister and mother." It is sad, but true that much suffering in this world has been caused by ethnic strife, by putting loyalty to family and clan and nation above loyalty to God. By his blood, Jesus will thin the blood loyalties so prevalent in our world, in order to create a new and united humanity that defines family, first and foremost, not by DNA, but by obedience to the will of God. This new family will not be identified by genealogy, but through baptism. In Jesus, water will become thicker than blood.

Questions

1) In the midst of the daily necessities and routine of life, it can be hard to have a larger vision of what God wants in the world. What gets in the way of that larger vision? In what ways can we be just like the religious leaders when it comes to Jesus?
2) Jesus intended for his followers to be a diverse group of people. While the global church is diverse, individual churches usually are not? Why is that?
3) Family is a wonderful thing, but family can get in the way of our faith journey. In what ways can family become a detriment to discipleship?

Chapter 4

Many years ago, when I was a young pastor, I received a telephone call from a parishioner one Sunday afternoon who wanted to speak with me about my sermon that morning. She informed me that something I said made her quite unhappy. I asked her to tell me what so bothered her. She began to relate to me the contentious words in question. As I listened, I began to wonder if she was listening to my sermon that morning or someone else's. What she heard resembled little of what I said, or at least intended to say.

When she was finished, I responded that if I had indeed said what she thought, I would be upset too. I apologized for my lack of communication that morning, and she in turn conceded that she may have been somewhat at fault in the hearing of my words.

The proclamation of the Word depends, not only upon the preacher, but upon the hearer. There will be those who will reject the truth being proclaimed no matter how poetic the preacher and convincing the argument. Others will receive the word gladly, only to allow the cares and frustrations of daily life to choke off the excitement.

Jesus comes proclaiming his Kingdom. The preacher and the message are the same. Yet throughout Mark, people receive his Word differently. It is an explosive message he proclaims, which is why he speaks in parables. Just as one cannot look directly into the sun, so the proclamation of God's Kingdom must be given in a kind of indirect speech, a kind of code language, a way of speaking about the things of God in a way that reflects the truth of the Kingdom, in the same way as one sees the sun be observing its rays shining on the grass and the trees. It is a radical message to those who believe that the Kingdom will come by violent power and might, and it is an extreme proclamation to persons who want to keep the Kingdom from coming. The former will reject Jesus' Kingdom message because of the way he says it is now breaking in; the latter because it threatens the status quo, the benefits of which they enjoy.

The Kingdom of God is surely here, but it does not come in the way the religious leaders and the masses expect. So, Jesus speaks of the Kingdom in ordinary ways with ordinary stories containing ordinary things. The Kingdom is like a growing seed, even a mustard seed. The disciples must pay attention to what is being said. The more they understand and the more they seek to understand, the more they will receive the benefits of the Kingdom. If they don't attend to the things that will deepen their faith, they will eventually lose what little they have. Grace is not an excuse to be lazy when it comes to discipleship.

Of course, Jesus not only spoke of the in-breaking Kingdom; he demonstrated that it was here. In the midst of a ferocious storm on Lake Galilee, the disciples, understandably so, are scared out of their wits. Jesus sees their fear as a lack of faith. If they understood his mission and if they truly believed that God was in control, they should have realized that his and their fate would not be tied to a storm at sea. Jesus speaks to the wind and the waves and everything becomes calm, but not just quiet; it was downright serene, "a dead calm," says the NRSV.

"Who then is this, that even the wind and the sea obey him?" Who is this indeed? He is one who is master of the elements that so often master humanity. No wonder Jesus can sleep in the back of the boat in the midst of the turmoil.

Questions

1) Communication can be difficult. What are some of the misconceptions of Jesus in the culture today?
2) Why do you think Jesus taught in parables? Do you find the parables easy to understand? Why or why not?
3) Jesus interprets the disciples fear on the Sea of Galilee as a lack of faith. Is all fear a lack of faith? Why or why not?

Chapter 5

One of the most popular movie franchises in the world is *Star Wars*. The numerous movies tell the story of a galactic struggle between the Empire and the Rebel Alliance. The tale moves back and forth between rebel victories and the response of the Empire. It is a cosmic struggle of epic proportions.

In Jesus' ministry, a cosmic war is being waged. Jesus is not simply a good teacher with some nice things to say; he is the champion who has come to rescue the world from the Principalities and Powers that hold creation and all of humanity in bondage.

In the region of the Gerasenes, Jesus and his disciples are in Gentile territory. In a scene right out of a Halloween nightmare, a demon-possessed man approaches Jesus. He was an individual who, no doubt struck fear into the hearts of those in the region. Living among the rocky tombs, perhaps inhabiting the places of burial that were empty, no one would go near him. Attempts to restrain him had failed. The inability to bind him reveals the severity of his bondage.

The demons inhabiting this tortured soul know exactly who this Jesus is. They may not be sure of the method by which Jesus has come to do battle with them, but they know his intentions. Even though they are wreaking havoc with this man's life and wreaking havoc with God's creation, they must still submit to this Lord of the wind and the waves.

The Legion of demons must obey Jesus' command to leave their host, but in not wanting to wander aimlessly across the earth, they ask for permission to inhabit a herd of pigs nearby.

One can hear the echo of Jewish purity in this moment—unclean spirits entering unclean swine.

The people are amazed that this man, who was so deranged, who ran among the tombs naked throwing himself on the ground in convulsions, is now sitting fully clothed and in his right mind. Jesus is able to do for him what no one else can. Surely the one who can calm the wind and the waves can calm tortured souls.

One would think that the witnesses to this amazing event would be rejoicing in this man's liberation, but apparently they become more afraid of Jesus than a possessed man living in the cemetery. Moreover, having just witnessed the local economy fall over the cliff, the people have seen enough of Jesus' liberating power.

"Jesus go away," they plead; and Jesus does. He will not stay where he is not wanted. God never coerces anyone into belief. God may woo, cajole, and move in ways to lead someone toward faith; but no one is ever forced into belief, as if that were even possible. Jesus will allow those who desire bondage to remain as they so want.

But there are those who truly want to be free, and who want their loved ones to be free. On the other side of the lake, Jairus, a leader of the synagogue, meets Jesus in a panic. His daughter is gravely ill. How is it possible to explain the terror of a parent who is in danger of losing a child? Unlike the disciples on the stormy lake, Jairus has faith in Jesus.

As they walk toward the house where the sick girl lay, an interruption takes place. Life is filled with interruptions, even in the midst of emergencies; but God uses emergencies and interruptions for his glory.

A woman ill for twelve years, who had spent all she on doctors who made her worse, quietly approaches Jesus in faith. She no doubt felt unworthy to approach Jesus face-to-face with a request for healing. Her internal bleeding made her ceremonially unclean, meaning that touching Jesus would make him unclean as well. What she discovers as she reaches out and touches the bottom of Jesus' cloak is that it is Jesus who makes all things and all persons clean.

Knowing that she has been found out, she approaches Jesus scared to death. One can imagine her fears subsiding when Jesus addresses her as "daughter." For so long, she has not felt as if she belonged to anyone. Her illness had isolated her from her family and from her community. She was not treated as a daughter of Abraham. But now as Jesus addresses her as such, she is reminded of her identity, of who she truly is in the eyes of God. Jesus restores her health and her status.

And now we discover that Jesus not only has power over demons and disease; he has power over the greatest of all enemies—death itself. The bad news comes to Jairus, "Dont trouble the teacher any further; your daughter is dead."

Death is all around. Even when Jesus enters the house, he is ridiculed for his seemly mistaken diagnosis. Those who laugh know death; they only know death. What they do not know, but will shortly, is that Jesus knows life. And as he raises this girl from the grip of the Grim Reaper, we discover that the Lord is concerned with all of human need. "Give her something to eat," he says.

Hunger, thirst, fear, death—Jesus has come to conquer them all.

Questions

1) Have you ever thought of the ministry of Jesus in terms of a cosmic struggle? If not, why not? If so, how does it feel to be part of something so big?
2) The Garasenes asked Jesus to leave them because of the miracle he did there. What are some reasons people today don't want to be bothered by Jesus?
3) Have you ever witnessed a miracle? How do you think you would react if you were present for one of Jesus' miracles?

Chapter 6

Years ago, I served as a chaplain for a small-town police department. One of the new officers grew up in the town. I will call him Edgar. In his youth, he was quite the hellion so town folk who knew him were rather surprised at his chosen profession.

I remember one night in particular while riding with him, we stopped a car speeding through town. As Edgar approached the vehicle and asked the driver for his license and registration, the occupant of the car recognized him and blurted out in a tone of unbelief, "Edgar, is that you? You're a cop?"

It may be true that knowledge brings respect, but it is also true that familiarity brings contempt. Jesus returns home. He is known by all; they have watched him grow into an adult, work at his father's trade, and then go off to wander around Israel as an itinerant prophet. Now he has returned home. They, who know him so well, or so it seems, cannot believe their ears as they listen to him teach.

They ask, "Isn't this Mary's son?" which is nothing more than a back-handed slap at his "illegitimate" origins, or so they think. How can this hometown boy they know so well, or so they believe, teach so profoundly, touch the human heart so deeply, and speak words of hope to those in such desperate need? They can't believe their ears, so they refuse to believe in him at all.

It is because of their lack of faith that Jesus chooses to do no mighty miracles in their midst. Why should he throw his pearls before swine? He heals a few who believe in him, despite the general consensus. Jesus is amazed at their lack of faith. Those who know him best should know who he is.

Jesus' hometown may not want to hear the Good News, but there are towns that do. Jesus now sends out the Twelve on their first evangelistic mission. They are to take nothing; they must rely completely on the hospitality of others—in short, they must rely completely on God to provide. The bag they are not to take is a beggar's bag. Even for the essentials, they must rely on others as well as work for their staples. Their mission is their work, and the hospitality they receive is a gracious and thankful response to God for the gift of the Good News proclaimed.

We are told that after their journey, they do mighty works in the name of their Lord. Clearly, they do not visit Nazareth.

Herod Antipas hears of Jesus and wonders if he is John the Baptist raised from the dead. Mark now moves into a brief interlude explaining how the Baptist met his fate. Prophets are often charged with speaking words of warning. John's words of condemnation land him in prison. While Herod would prefer not to execute John, he has no choice. Fooled by the wiles of his wife, and pushed into the corner by his own lust, he has John beheaded.

After the Interlude is over, Mark returns us to Jesus and his activities. The Twelve report to Jesus all that has happened on their missionary journey. Jesus attempts to give them some time to rest. The exhilaration of ministry leads to exhaustion. If the disciples are to continue to be in effective service to their Lord, they need time to sleep and rejuvenate; but it is not to be. The crowd is relentless in their pursuit of Jesus. No wonder they seem like lost sheep without a shepherd. Not only are they without a shepherd, they are searching for one and believe they have found him.

Human need is not found only in the periodic frailties that confront men, women, and children, but it extends to the daily necessities as well. The people are hungry. In the miraculous feeding of the five thousand, Jesus attends to a daily need. "Give us this day our daily bread." Jesus is more than able to do so, and not only that; there are leftovers. God gives in abundance. Is it any wonder that the people see this provider of heavenly manna as the prophet like Moses spoken of in the Scriptures?

Now it is definitely time for rest and for prayer. Jesus makes his disciples get into the boat. Later that evening while Jesus is praying and the disciples are in the boat off shore, in the midst of difficult winds, Jesus approaches the disciples walking on the water. The disciples are certain that they are witnessing a specter coming in their direction, and they are, in typical human fashion, terrified.

Jesus calls out to them in order to assuage their fears. As he gets into the boat they are "utterly astounded." Why? Mark tells us because "they did not understand about the loaves." They still did not realize that in Jesus God was doing something new and that they were called to be part of it. Why should they fear? Just as Moses saw the people safely to the Promised Land, so Jesus, the one who provides new manna, will see them safely through their mission. Why would Jesus allow them to perish with their work still incomplete? The time will come when they will pass from this life to the next, but for now, as long as Jesus is with them, all will be well.

As soon as Jesus and the Twelve reach shore, the crowd is there. Any solitude they may have had is now over. At times, it seems as if there is no rest for the righteous.

Questions

1) Some people's conversions to Christianity can be a surprise to others. Do you know any Christians whose way of life was transformed radically by their acceptance of Jesus?
2) What do you think Mark means by "they did not understand about the loaves?"
3) After reading the first six chapters of Mark, what are you learning about Jesus and his connection to the Old Testament?

Chapter 7

I know a man who is an exceedingly careful driver. He has never had a speeding ticket because he is vigilant never to drive over the speed limit. In fact, he is so careful that he makes it point to drive five miles under the limit posted. Needless, to say, he is an irritant to those driving behind him. When I asked him how he felt about angering those behind him, he just said, "I've never had a ticket."

When the Israelites returned from Babylonian Exile, they were so committed to refraining from the idolatry their ancestors had committed by not keeping the Law of Moses, they put a "fence" around the Law, that is they formulated rules even stricter than the Law itself. They reasoned quite logically that if someone did not cross the "fence" of stricter regulations, she or he would certainly not violate the Law. The problem was that over time the "fence" had come to be viewed as a violation of the Law itself.

Time and time again in his ministry, Jesus shows that he is quite unconcerned with adherence to that "fence," what he will refer to as the Pharisees' "traditions." The Pharisees question Jesus on this in reference to the disciples' lack of scruples in eating with "unwashed hands," hands that are ceremonially unclean. It is interesting to note that they do not implicate Jesus in this practice. It could be they are not-so-subtly suggesting that Jesus, as his followers' rabbi, is leading his disciples astray, which is indeed a serious charge. It may explain, at least in part, why Jesus responds to the Pharisees in anger.

The purpose of the "fence" around the Law was originally meant to preserve the Law, but over time it had taken its place as equal to the Law. Thus, in the eyes of Jesus, it nullified the Law given to Moses. When the "fence" around the Law was used to neglect the weightier matters of the Law, such as care of the orphan and the widow, the protection of the powerless, and elderly parents, then that "fence" designed to safeguard the people from idolatry, in actuality led them into it. If the Pharisees were accusing Jesus of leading his disciples astray, Jesus countered that they, the religious leadership, were guilty of sending the entire nation of Israel over a cliff.

In majoring in the minors, the Pharisees had forgotten the true purpose of the Law of Moses; they had neglected what truly matters. The Pharisees were more concerned with ritual washings before meals and exactly what kinds of food were consumed. But for Jesus, cleanliness before God consisted not in these things, but in what came from the human heart. While human beings tend to lose their focus on what is significant, Jesus always gets to the heart of the matter. Perhaps, human beings try to avoid what is central because focusing on the peripheral is less disarming and calls for less change and less accountability.

Having declared that the heart is the heart of the matter, Jesus now demonstrates this in his ministry to a woman not of Jewish lineage. It was common in Judaism to refer to Gentiles as "dogs." In a time before canines were domesticated, dogs ran in packs; they were wild and created trouble, and searched only to fulfill their own hungers. For many Jews in Jesus' day, this was an apt description of those not descended from Abraham.

So, Jesus' response to the Syro-Phoenician woman when she asks for healing for her daughter, is not surprising in that context; what is unexpected is her response. "OK," she says, "what you say may be true, that the promises of the God of Israel are reserved first for Israel's children, but just as dogs manage to get some scraps of food reserved for the children, perhaps my daughter might receive some benefit from what is not reserved for her."

Time and time again, we find examples of persons in the Gospels who display the kind of profound faith that surpasses those who have been entrusted with the oracles of God. Such faith from the supposed "dogs" always impressed Jesus.

News about Jesus continues to spread. When he heals a man with hearing and speech impediments, Jesus orders that no one tell the good news of what is happening. How does one unable to talk, and who can now speak keep silent about what has happened to him?

The people affirm that Jesus continues to do everything well.

Questions

1) While most agree that following rules is generally a good thing, where have you seen people, like the Pharisees' putting a stricter fence around rules that are not good?
2) Jesus accused the Pharisees of majoring in minors. Where do Christians major in the minors today?
3) Why do you think Jesus told the formerly deaf man not to tell anyone about his healing?

Chapter 8

Years ago, my wife and I were driving to the beach in South Carolina. I needed to get gas, but had yet to stop hoping for a better price. Our GPS took us the most direct way (at least according to the GPS) and we found ourselves on a long stretch of desolate road with cotton fields on both sides. The warning light came on indicating we were almost out of fuel. I started imagining walking on that desolate highway for miles trying to find a filling station. Our dashboard indicated we had about ten miles of gas left in the tank, when ahead of us on the corner of an all but empty intersection was a small gas station. I hadn't experienced that kind of relief in a long time.

The crowd is once again in a desolate place, and Jesus is concerned with their physical well-being. In several places the Hebrew Scriptures promise that God's future salvation will make the desert blossom. Just as God supplied food to the people in the wilderness of Sinai, so the people of Israel looked forward to the day when God would bring a new Exodus of deliverance that would supply an abundance. The miracle of feeding the masses from a few loaves of bread and some fish was a sign that the hope of Israel was now being fulfilled in Jesus.

The disciples had witnessed the feeding of the five thousand; one might have hoped that they would, by this time, understand that what Jesus had done once, he could do again. But they respond as if Jesus has performed no miracle before. "How can one feed these people with bread here in the desert?"

Before distributing the bread and the fish, Jesus gives thanks. "Blessed are you Lord our God, King of the Universe, who brings forth bread from the earth." The substance of the everyday is to be received in thanksgiving, not simply in experiencing the miraculous, nor only when God protects from disaster.

As to be expected the people eat until they are satisfied, and there are leftovers. As Jesus sends the crowd away, he immediately (there's that word again) gets into a boat with his disciples, to seek a quiet place.

Such is, once again, not to be the case. The Pharisees, who have already made up their minds about Jesus come to him asking for a sign. It is irrelevant that Jesus has performed many signs. They have already decided that Jesus is an imposter, and nothing will deter them from their disbelief in Jesus. But Jesus is not at the Pharisees' beck and call. His signs are glimpses of the coming Kingdom and performed for the benefit of humanity. Jesus is not some snake-oil salesman performing the incredible for people who just want to see a show, nor is he interested in doing the miraculous for those who desire to prove him to be a charlatan.

Jesus' warning to the disciples over the yeast (the evil) of the Pharisees and the Herodians is misunderstood by them as a rebuke for forgetting to bring more bread with them on the boat. Jesus' exasperation is clearly revealed. After all they have been through with him, after what they have seen and witnessed, they still do not get that since Jesus is God's Anointed; he will provide what they need.

After the healing of a blind man in the town of Bethsaida, Jesus asks the disciples what the rumors are about concerning his identity. Human beings love to speculate, and there was no end of speculation as to who Jesus was. Knowing that the disciples must answer that question as well, he asks them, "But who do you say that I am." Peter responds, "You are the Messiah." He knows the name, but has yet to learn the content of that name. When Jesus attempts to explain to the disciples what it means for him to be the Messiah, Peter, acting like Jesus' superior begins to correct his misunderstanding in a condescending way.

Jesus now feels the need to instruct the disciples and the crowd on what true discipleship means. Jesus, the suffering servant will pave the way for salvation by his suffering and death, but those who would follow should not assume that the way of discipleship is all sweetness and light. The way of the cross is for those who would follow as well; it is a walking in the footsteps of the Master.

For those who are too ashamed to be identified with the scandalous message of Jesus' way will find themselves on the receiving end of such shame when Judgment Day arrives.

Questions

1) In feeding the masses, Jesus demonstrates concern for people's physical well-being. Has the church at times neglected the physical needs of others in favor of only a spiritual interpretation of the gospel?
2) Even though the religious leaders have witnessed Jesus perform miracles, they still ask for a sign. Why do you think they refused to believe in Jesus in spite of his miraculous works?
3) Peter believed in Jesus as the Savior, but it is clear from the Gospels he failed to understand how Jesus would save. What did Peter miss and what do twenty-first century followers of Jesus still miss today?

Chapter 9

Have you ever caught a glimpse of something wonderful? Perhaps it's a preview of what looks to be a good movie? Maybe it's that call back for a second interview for the dream job you've always wanted? How about the positive pregnancy test, an indicator of the new life to be born?

What must the disciples have heard when Jesus tells them, "Truly I tell you, there are some standing here who will not taste death until they see that the kingdom of God has come with power" (9:1). Possibly there was a sense of excitement that Jesus was finally going to make his move, leading a revolt against Pilate and his minions. Perhaps now, at long last, God was going to reign in Jerusalem and the disciples would be major power-players in the kingdom.

Instead, three of the disciples glimpse the kingdom in a way they are simply not expecting. In Mount Sinai fashion, Jesus takes Peter, James, and John to a high mountain. In what is surely best described as an ancient fireworks show, Jesus appears before them in a dazzling and holy white appearance along with Moses and Elijah. Moses prophesied that one would come after him who would be reminiscent of his ministry. Elijah would return to proclaim the coming of the Messiah. The three of them talk. Mark gives us no details, but Luke hints that the discussion concerns coming events in Jerusalem.

Peter, who never seems to be at a loss for silly words, suggests that the six of them just make a lifetime of it on top of the mountain. Of course, he is terrified, so there is some sense in which his response is understandable. Peter once again cannot embrace the fact that, in his association with Jesus, he is part of something he simply cannot control. Instead of just resigning himself to go along for the ride, he feels the need to put his own personal stamp on unfolding events.

The imagery from the Scriptures is so thick, one wonders how the disciples could have missed the point. The mountain, Moses and Elijah, the cloud, and the voice, should be understood as the validation of Jesus' mission. We do not know what they made of their mountaintop experience, but Jesus orders them to tell no one until after he has been raised from the dead, a comment whose meaning they perplex over among themselves.

Mountaintop experiences cannot last forever. Peter may have wanted to stay up and away from the fray, but Jesus has come precisely to impose himself into the suffering and pain of the world, which is exactly what they find at the bottom of the mountain. A father has brought his boy suffering from a demon to the nine disciples at the bottom of the hill, but they are unable to cure him. Jesus, in his frustration refers to the faithlessness of the disciples. How important it is to note that the Lord refers not to the lack of faith of the one in need of healing, but the ones through whom God wants to heal.

The father, however, seems to have his own fragile faith, perhaps because of the failure of the nine. He says to Jesus, "... if you are able to do anything, have pity on us and help us." The father responds to Jesus' surprised reaction with some of the most significant words in the Bible revealing the human condition of uncertainty: "I believe; help my unbelief!"

With his son healed, Jesus and his disciples move on to Capernaum. Jesus wants to know what they were arguing about as they traveled. They were silent in response for good reason. Perhaps the three disciples who had been on the mountain with Jesus, who had privileged information about what they experienced, were lording it over the other nine. An argument ensues over which one of them will be the greatest in the kingdom. They know better than to tell Jesus what they were discussing. Jesus' own life and ministry has been an exercise in servanthood and sacrifice, and they are still pushing and shoving each other verbally over their top-dog status.

Jesus, knowing the content of their discussion reminds them of the upside-down nature of greatness in God's kingdom. It is doubtful that Jesus' words make any sense to the disciples. At some point, later on, they will understand as they will walk a road reminiscent of their master; but for now, they continue to ponder, wonder, reflect, and still basically get it wrong in understanding who this Jesus is and what he is about in his mission to Israel and the world.

Questions

1) Scholars are not in agreement about what Jesus means when he says to his followers "some standing here will not taste death until they see that the kingdom of God has come with power." What do you think he means?
2) Why are Moses and Elijah important to Jesus' ministry? Why did they appear with him and not some other Old Testament figures?
3) Mark tells us that Jesus' disciples could not heal because they lacked faith. How do we show a lack of faith in Jesus?

Chapter 10

There's an old joke about the couple who were inactive members of their church. They only showed up for Christmas and Easter and rarely assisted with any of the church ministries.

One day they received a letter from the pastor. The husband reads the letter and says to his wife who is curious about its content, "It's bad news. We're being summoned for active duty."

Commitment is serious business. Throughout his ministry Jesus has dealt with those committed in a half-hearted way. Jesus understands the demanding nature of discipleship, so he insists that would-be followers count the cost before they decide to commit themselves.

Commitment is serious business in all other relationships as well. Some Pharisees approach Jesus asking if it is lawful for a man to divorce his wife, interjecting Jesus right into the middle of a hot debate in his day over what grounds constitute a lawful divorce. Once again Jesus is not simply going to allow the conversation to be framed within the conventional wisdom of the day. He goes behind the law; he digs below the surface of regulations in order to uncover motives and to expose truths that others prefer were left buried.

For Jesus, the issue is not about what makes for a just divorce, but what makes for a committed relationship. Jesus says to the Pharisees, "It was because your hearts were hard that Moses wrote you this law... what God has joined together, let no one separate." Commitment is serious business.

After blessing some children and rebuking his disciples for turning them away, Jesus is once again questioned on legal details, this time in reference to the inheritance of eternal life. Once again, Jesus mines beneath the surface of the question. It is not only a matter of keeping the Ten Commandments, it is about embodying the ways of God in one's life, which can only be done as those things that separate women and men from God are removed from their desires. What separated this man from his eternity was his great wealth and Jesus knew it. Jesus' love for the man led Jesus to speak the difficult truth to him. "One thing you lack. Go, sell everything you have and give it to the poor, and you will have treasure in heaven. Then come, follow me."

It must not be overlooked, as it sometimes is, that Jesus is not demanding that the rich man rid himself of all his earthly possessions to live destitute on the street. In actuality, Jesus is inviting the young man to begin a different journey. For so long his journey had been focused on the pursuit of wealth, but Jesus invites the man to join him on a journey in the pursuit of God.

The rich man turns away unwilling to part with what he obviously loved more than God. Commitment is serious business.

For those who make such a commitment, God will surely reward them. In God's Great Reversal, the first will be last and the last will be first. The rich will become poor and the poor will become rich. Jesus once again reminds the disciples that the way to resurrection will come through the cross; the road to victory will be paved with Jesus' suffering and death.

Yet in typical fashion, the disciples continue not to get it. James and John approach with a request along the old order of things. They ask for the two most prestigious seats in Jesus'

Kingdom—the Secretary of State and the Secretary of the Treasury. The other ten disciples are angry with James and John, likely not because they had the audacity to ask Jesus for these high offices, but because James and John had trumped the rest of them by asking first. Jesus must have been quite irritated in having, once again, to instruct them on the upside-down nature of the Kingdom of God, as opposed to the ways of the kingdoms of the world. "Whoever wants to become great among you must be your servant, and whoever wants to be first must be slave of all."

And as a reminder that Jesus' words, though difficult to accept, do indeed depict the true nature of his Kingdom, Jesus gives sight to blind Bartimaeus. And unlike the rich young man who turns away from Jesus, Bartimaeus follows immediately along the way. Having been healed, he realizes that there are truly no other options for him. Whatever this journey will require of him, he must follow. Commitment is serious business.

Questions

1) What practices demonstrate that we are seriously committed to Jesus?
2) Jesus invites the rich man to a different journey. How has Jesus made your faith journey different?
3) Jesus presents leadership in his kingdom as an upside-down triangle. Those at the top are the greatest and most humble, and the ones the world puts at the top with all the wealth and power are of the least importance. If today's leaders attempted to embody that kind of reversed way of leading, how would it look?

Chapter 11

Have you ever been told you remind people of someone else? Perhaps you have a doppelganger—a look alike—somewhere? I've been told I look like a famous baseball player (long retired) and a certain actor whose name I will not mention. Since I have an identical twin brother, I remind others of him and he of me.

Jesus now enters Jerusalem one last time and the way he enters will be reminiscent of a previous Jewish hero. No doubt the people are reminded of another triumphal entry many decades before—the entry of Judas Maccabeus, who had liberated Jerusalem from the Syrians and cleansed the Temple. But Jesus has something else in mind for the Temple. He will spend the next several days needling the religious authorities to within an inch of their patience.

The people come out to greet Jesus as he enters the city. It is quite the spontaneous parade. His first stop upon his arrival is the Temple itself, but it is too late in the day, so Jesus leaves for Bethany with his disciples to stay with friends.

The next day, Jesus performs a strange act that will explain his soon-to-be-actions in the Temple. Jesus is hungry, so he approaches a fig tree to pick some of its fruit, even though Jesus knows that its season for the production of fruit has already passed. Nevertheless, he curses the fig tree saying, "May no one ever eat fruit from you again."

He then enters the Temple to do what he had planned to do the night before, but did not because the hustle and bustle of the day had finished. In an act sure to get everybody's attention,

Jesus begins turning over the tables of the money changers and those selling animals for sacrifice, refusing to allow anyone to carry anything through.

Jesus' anger is two-fold with both concerns related. The religious leaders have taken the Temple, which God had intended to be a place for all the nations to come and worship, and they had crowded out the Gentiles with their buying and selling. They had turned the Temple into a place of ethnic pride and exclusivity.

Moreover, in so doing the religious leaders had also turned the Temple, says Jesus quoting Jeremiah, into their own little safety zone, their refuge, feeling that they are safe from God's judgment. In essence, Jesus accuses them of turning the Temple into the hideout where they, "the James Gang," divide the loot they have robbed from others.

In this symbolic act, Jesus does not cleanse the Temple; he judges it. The Saducees and the Pharisees have so corrupted the Temple, that there is no reforming it. God will judge it, just as Jesus cursed the fig tree. If the tree will not bear fruit in its season, then there will be no season for it at all. God has expected his people, his fig tree, to bear fruit and they have not; so now the season for producing fruit has passed and there will be no further opportunities.

Such acts continue to raise the authority question in the minds of the religious leaders. The chief priests and the scribes and the elders ask Jesus, "By what authority are you doing these things. Who gave you authority to do them."

Of course, there is nothing that Jesus can say that will satisfy them, so he turns the tables on them by asking them a question: "Did John's baptism come from heaven or from human origin?" They know that no matter how they answer, they have a problem. They did not believe John, but they knew that the people believed him to be a prophet. How often it is true that the "laity" are more in tune with the things of God than the "clergy."

Instead of taking a stand they simply respond that they do not know; an amazing admission from people who are supposed to know these things. Jesus responds to them in like fashion. If they will not answer his question, neither will he answer theirs. At this point, the religious leaders are probably so embarrassed that they do not press Jesus further. At least in this they are wise.

Questions

1) Jesus' triumphal entry has been called a symbolic act. What was Jesus symbolizing and why is the symbolic important?
2) Jesus indicates that the religious leaders have so corrupted the Temple and its practices that reform is no longer possible. Is there a time to give up on something or someone ever changing?
3) What did the religious leaders have the most to lose in allowing Jesus to continue his ministry?

Chapter 12

There are events in life that take us by surprise. Other things that happen seem inevitable. In my younger days, I had a friend who lived hard. He drank and used drugs and he drove his motorcycle fast. His friends who cared for him kept warning that he was headed for disaster if he didn't change his ways.

One day it happened. While riding his motorcycle and no doubt under the influence, he wrecked his bike off the side of the road. He was lucky to have survived, but he severely broke his legs. I remember visiting him in the hospital with a cast on both legs up to his waste. My tough, often emotionless friend, was in tears from the pain. All of us who knew him were not surprised that his life had come to this.

Jesus now comes into direct conflict with the religious authorities. This is no surprise. It is the inevitable outcome of his teaching and his criticism of the authorities. He tells a parable about a vineyard and those who were given the task of caring for it. Instead of being good stewards of the vineyard making it productive on behalf of the owner, the tenants desire to have the vineyard for themselves, even resorting to killing the owner's son. Yet, in spite of this, the tenants are no match for the owner; he will take his vineyard back and throw out the caretakers who have been so careless and corrupt.

When Jesus is done telling his story, the implications are obvious. The religious leaders know he is speaking against them. God entrusted them with his vineyard (Israel) and they have mismanaged and failed to be responsible with their charge. Here the actions of Jesus in the Temple come back into view.

God still owns the vineyard and will tend to it, but those who have been placed over it will be removed; but not before they kill the Son of God.

The chief priests, the scribes, and the elders want to arrest Jesus, but he is still quite popular with the masses. They leave, but they are not gone for good.

It is now their turn to test Jesus in the hope of leveling a charge against him. Some Pharisees and Herodians come to him in order "to trap him." Pharisees and Herodians did not get along. They were polar opposites in many ways; but as it is said, politics makes strange bedfellows. We were reminded earlier in Mark's story that at times the enemy of my enemy is my friend.

The Pharisees and the Herodians begin with empty flattery: "Teacher, we know that you are sincere, and show deference to no one; for you do not regard people with partiality." Jesus, of course, is not taken in by their empty words. Nevertheless, the question they ask Jesus is politically charged. 'Is it lawful to pay taxes to the emperor or not?"

They appear to have Jesus in a no-win situation. If he tells them to pay the tax, then he risks losing his following among his fellow Jews, who despise the tax and see it as a compromise with paganism. If Jesus recommends withholding the tax, then they have something to charge him with before Pilate. It is interesting to note that Jesus does not have the coin in question, but those who ask the question do, revealing their own hypocrisy.

As the image of Caesar is on the coin, says Jesus, give it to Caesar; but you give yourself to God. Jesus is not saying that he likes the tax, but neither is he suggesting that the Jews start a tax revolt, which would bring the wrath of Rome down upon him.

The imagery of images is clear. The coin that is in Caesar's image should be given to Caesar; but human beings, who are in the image of God, need to give themselves completely to God. Faithfulness to God, reflecting God's image in the world and to those around, even in undesirable circumstances is what God requires.

It could be that there is a reminder here of the parable of the vineyard. Jesus has accused the religious authorities of not reflecting God's image in the world, and perhaps that is the suggestion here as well.

More testing for Jesus is now at hand. The Pharisees and the Herodians have been unsuccessful in tripping up Jesus. It is now the Sadducees' turn. They approach Jesus with the question concerning the resurrection. They really do not care what Jesus believes about husbands and wives in eternity. What they want to know is whether or not Jesus believes in the resurrection of the dead at all.

Mark tells us that the Sadducees did not believe in the resurrection of the dead. This was just not an abstract theological debate amongst scholars who disagreed; the debate over the resurrection of the dead was just as politically charged as the argument over paying taxes to Caesar. The Sadducees rejected resurrection, among other reasons because resurrection subversively suggested that God was going to bring renewal, that God was eventually going to topple kingdoms, including Rome. Those who have a stake in the status quo, who benefit from things staying the same, do not need God coming to rain on their parade.

Quoting from the Book of Exodus, which is found in the Pentateuch (the first five books of the Old Testament), which were the only books the Sadducees accepted as Scripture, Jesus affirms his belief in this politically subversive doctrine. Of course, most of Jesus' fellow Jews believe in resurrection as well, so while there can be no charge for which to accuse Jesus, at least, they know where he stands.

After Jesus is given one more question concerning the greatest commandment, and he in turn denounces the scribes, Jesus and his disciples behold the sight of the very wealthy putting in large sums of money into the Temple treasury. After them comes a very poor and elderly widow, who deposits two of the least valuable coins possible; an amount that will obviously go unnoticed as the money is counted.

But Jesus notices; in fact, he responds to this act by telling his disciples something that they found hard to believe. "Truly I tell you, this poor widow has put in more than all those who are contributing to the treasury. For all of them have contributed out of their abundance, but she out of her poverty has put in everything she had, all she had to live on."

The contrast cannot be seen more clearly, not only in reference to the wealthy contributing their leftovers, but in contradistinction to the religious authorities throughout the chapter, who unlike this widow, have failed to be faithful, even though God has entrusted them with much. She in her poverty has pleased God; she is a faithful part of the vineyard that God loves.

Questions

1) In the parable of the vineyard, Jesus is telling the religious leaders a brutal truth about themselves they cannot receive. Why is the difficult truth hard for us to hear?
2) When Jesus tells the authorities to give to Caesar what is his, and to God what is God's, he is not promoting the separation of church and state as some have proposed. There was no such idea in the first-century world. What do you think Jesus means by this statement?
3) In Jesus' day, giving was a public thing. People knew how much others gave to the Temple and the synagogue. Is it a good idea to know what other people give to the church and/or charity? Why do we keep such matters private today?

Chapter 13

Have you ever been told something you find difficult to believe? "I saw Bigfoot!" says a friend. You believe that she witnessed something because you know your friend is a truthful person, but you are certain that she must have seen something else.

I suspect Jesus' disciples had trouble believing what he tells them in this chapter. The temple and its complex in Jerusalem must have been one incredible sight as it stood majestically on Mount Zion. Being at the center of Israel's faith, the building elicited pride in faithful Jews. Such is the perspective of the disciples, who point out to Jesus the obvious as they call his attention to the massive buildings and the extremely large stones that comprise the structures.

So, it must have been quite a jolt for the disciples to hear Jesus' response. "Do you see these great buildings? Not one stone will be left here upon another; all will be thrown down." Of course, the disciples want to know the signs of these events. Perhaps they think such a destruction will signify the end of the world. Jesus is not referring to the end of the world, but the destruction of the temple in 70 A.D. For Jesus, the eschatological end of the age was not yet to come; it had already arrived. This does not mean that Jesus believed that 70 A.D. marked the end of the world, but that the destruction of Jerusalem meant the end of "the world of early Judaism as a temple-centered faith".[2] Jesus had already symbolically pronounced God's judg-

---

2 Ben Witherington III, *The Gospel of Mark*, (Grand Rapids, MI: Wm B Eerdmans, 2001), p. 340.

ment upon the temple in driving the money changers from its precincts; now Jesus points to its actual destruction, which he views as God's judgment, not only on the temple, but upon Jerusalem and the religious leadership.

But Jesus also has a larger picture of God's judgment in mind. Wars and rumors of wars and nation rising against nation, etc. reflect the much larger portrait of the judgment of the world. Although Jesus' words primarily concern events to take place within forty years, there is also a larger view to the end when the Son of Man comes to judge and to redeem. It must never be forgotten that judgment is redemptive and that redemption involves judgment.

It is critical to note that the signs Jesus' gives his disciples are general and vague and always contemporary. War and suffering, famine and earthquakes, persecutions and false Messiahs have not only been prevalent throughout history; they are also to be witnessed and experienced in the present, and they will be encountered in the future. Thus, the posture that Jesus is encouraging his disciples to take is not one where such signs signal the imminent end of history, but rather that such events remind them of the necessity to be ready for the end because they cannot know from these signs when it will take place.

Just what does it mean to be ready for the end? It does not involve engaging in eschatological or end times weather forecasting by attempting to put these general signs to specific, contemporary events and people. Rather readiness is revealed in the church being about the business of the kingdom. Watchful Christians are faithful Christians who attend to the work Christ has given them.

The Second Coming of Christ is in the hands of the Father. The signs Jesus gives do not reveal clues as to when this will all take place; on the contrary, they remind us that we have no idea when it will happen. Christians are not to engage in such speculation, but in proclamation and mission because in Jesus God is doing a new thing that will usher people into the new world of salvation. We do not know when history will end, but we do know, that with the first coming of Christ we are now in the eschatological age, the last act of the drama of history, in which the final curtain will fall in the Divine Director's own good time.

Questions

1) The disciples could not imagine the destruction of the Temple. It would have meant the end of their world. What events today lead people to believe the end of the world is near?
2) The belief in God's judgment is not a popular notion today, but Jesus does mention it more than once. C.S. Lewis refers to God's judgment as letting us have what we want. Do you agree with Lewis? If not, how would you define the judgment of God?
3) Many human beings are fascinated by the future and want to know what will take place. Why is that? What does it mean to trust God for the future?

Chapter 14

"He's trying to get rid of me," she confided while we sat in my office at the church. She was employed at a small business. I will name her "Marge." Her job was to work with the accounts. Marge discovered some irregularities and in investigating more fully, she realized that the owner—who was also a longtime friend—was skimming money off the top and stealing from clients. Since Marge was a friend, she did not go to the authorities, but approached her boss informing him of what she found and pleaded with him to make it right. Instead of taking her advice, he started to look for a way to get rid of her without calling attention to what he had done. Needless to say, Marge was in a difficult situation.

Jesus is in a difficult situation. There are those looking to get rid of Jesus. In cleansing the Temple, Jesus has pronounced God's judgment upon it. For the religious leadership this was the final straw. They now look for a way to kill him, but given that the Passover is upon them, they need to exercise caution; messianic fervor and national pride is running high, and the last thing the chief priests and the teachers of the law want is an uprising that will result in a Roman crackdown.

Jesus is still in Bethany, a stone's throw from Jerusalem. As he is enjoying table fellowship, a woman enters the room and anoints Jesus' head. The outrageous act is received as such by those gathered at the table. "Some of those present were saying indignantly to one another, 'Why this waste of perfume? It could have been sold for more than a year's wages and the money given to the poor' And they rebuked her harshly." How often people will oppose spending money on something and use feeding the poor as justification. It is not so much that they are so concerned about the poor; they simply oppose what has happened.

Like so many during the ministry of Jesus, their response is simply an exercise in missing the point. "The poor you will always have with you," says Jesus. This is not an excuse not to care for the hungry; indeed, it is a reminder of the poverty that demands the attention of those who would be obedient to God. Yet, in her act this woman has borne witness to what God is doing and going to do in this Jesus. She does not know all the details of what God is going to accomplish, but she recognizes that he is the focus of God's plan and that these moments in the presence of Jesus are divine moments which must be savored. Jesus must be given his due honor. Her act is an act of love and devotion that foreshadows, unbeknownst to her, Jesus' death.

As Jesus gathered for the Passover meal with his disciples and others, emotions and spirits were no doubt conflicted. The joy of the Passover celebration was tempered by the rising tensions swirling in the air around Jesus. Any joy was squelched when Jesus announced, "I tell you the truth, one of you will betray me—one who is eating with me." To be willing to have table fellowship with one you are about to turn in is an egregious breach of hospitality customs in the first century Jewish world. It is bad enough to betray Jesus, but for the betrayer to sit at the table with Jesus in "friendship" is dastardly to say the least. Before the meal ends, Jesus will take the Passover meal and its centuries old ritual, and transform it into something that will echo through the centuries in a uniquely Christian way.

Betrayal is not the only thing on the mind of Jesus; denial is close at hand as well. Simon Peter, whose verbal bravado throughout the Gospels is louder and more courageous than his follow-through, insists that he will go to the death for Jesus. The other disciples, in like fashion, promise the same. How disheartening it must have been for Jesus to know that in the last hours of his life, the men he spent most of his waking moments with would abandon him in his greatest hour of need. Moreover, the disciples' desertion would be made all the worse by their inability to stay awake in the Garden of Gethsemane. Surely by now they know that things have become quite serious, and that the climactic moment is at hand; and yet, while Jesus prays in torment, Peter, James, and John cannot even keep their eyes open.

As Jesus is arrested, one of the disciples attempts to defend him cutting off the ear of the servant of the high priest. Jesus rejects such a response. He has refused to lead a violent revolt throughout his ministry, and he will not resort to it now even when threatened. Perhaps for the disciples, this is the final confirmation for them that Jesus will not be the kind of Messiah they desire. Here Jesus rejects, for one final time, what the disciples have desperately wanted him to do; here is where he can take his stand against Rome. He does not.

As Jesus stands before the Sanhedrin, the religious ruling council, the outcome of the trial has already been decided before it is over, and Jesus' response ensures the outcome the high priest desires. They begin to strike him and make fun of him, no doubt a painful affair for Jesus; but even more painful for him is what is happening out in the courtyard while Jesus is being beaten. Jesus' words to Peter are coming true as his number one disciple not only denies him three times, but swears a divine oath in affirmation of his ignorance, not only lying to those around him, but doing so in the name of the Divine One who is truth.

The rooster crows a final time and Peter responds in the only way appropriate for such profane perjury; he breaks down and sobs inconsolably.

Questions

1) The woman's anointing of Jesus with expensive perfume is perceived as a waste of money. Where does the church spend money today that is not a waste, but viewed as such?
2) Jesus says that the women's act of anointing was an act of extravagant generosity. In what ways can we be extravagantly generous to Jesus today?
3) Peter verbally denied knowing Jesus. What are the ways in which Christians deny or at least hide being believers today?

Chapter 15

I was summoned for jury duty. On the day I reported, I sat in the courtroom with approximately thirty other people waiting to be examined along with everybody else to see who would be seated and who sent home. After what seemed like a long time, the presiding judge came in to tell us that the plaintiff and defendant had settled out of court at the last minute. The judge informed us that it was not all that uncommon for the two sides in question to come to an agreement at the last minute when they witnessed prospective jurors arriving to be interviewed. It was at that moment of realization that this was serious business and they stood to lose their case completely. A compromise was to be preferred to a complete loss. Settlement became the preferred outcome.

Jesus' trial is serious business. He is taken to Pilate, who questions Jesus, but Jesus makes no reply. Perhaps Jesus fulfills Isaiah's prophecy in remaining silent; in addition, Jesus has no reason to defend himself before Pilate or anyone else for that matter. He is accused of treason. In one sense, this may be a false accusation, since he has no interest in leading a revolt against Rome. Yet, anyone who proclaims the coming of God's Kingdom threatens the powers that be in this world. In one sense, Pilate may see Jesus as no threat; in another sense, he brings into question any who rule apart from God's reign.

In keeping with his Passover custom, Pilate is willing to release Jesus if the people desire. It is entirely possible that Pilate would like to see Jesus freed simply to stick his finger in the eye of Caiaphas, whom Pilate despises. But the crowd wants nothing to do with Jesus. Perhaps the many who had followed Jesus have come to realize that the liberation he offers will leave Pilate in charge. If Jesus refuses to be the Messiah they desire him to be, it is better to release Barabbas; someone who, in brigand-like fashion has demonstrated in no uncertain terms what he is willing to do in order to liberate God's people through violence.

"Crucify him! Crucify him!" The crowd shouts in a fashion that echoes through the centuries, speaking for all who have sinned and fallen short of God's glory. And although Pilate would like to be exonerated of his complicity, he too is also responsible for Jesus' death. No one is innocent.

Once Pilate hands down the order for Jesus' death, the guards, more-than-expertly trained in the gruesome art of crucifixion, take over. There are no rules laid upon them. There is no debating as to what constitutes torture. The only thing they need to make sure of is that they do not kill Jesus before he can be nailed to the cross. The Romans want to make sure that the people witness Jesus' fate in order to deter others from leading a band of revolutionaries.

In leading Jesus to Calvary, he is simply not capable of carrying the cross-beam to the hill of his death. They enlist a passer-by, who is simply minding his own business, to carry the cross for Jesus. How true it is that the random elements of life can change human beings forever. We know nothing of Simon of Cyrene, other than the fact that he was coming into Jerusalem from the country. What we can perhaps surmise is that somehow this unexpected event for Simon changed his life forever; for Mark connects Simon to his sons, who were known by Mark's audience. Perhaps Alexander and Rufus are followers of Jesus because their father, Simon became a follower of Jesus?

As Jesus hangs upon the cross, the people say, "He saved others, but he can't save himself." This is not a surprise to those who truly know Jesus. It would be impossible for Jesus to save others if he saved himself from death. He tried to tell his disciples, and all would listen to him, of the sacrificial nature of God himself. But since they cannot understand what it means to lose one's life in order to find it, they simply resort to hurling insults upon him until he dies.

Joseph of Arimathea approaches Pilate asking for Jesus' body. It may be that Pilate grants the request as one more way to irritate Caiaphas. Instead of throwing Jesus' body to the dogs and birds by the side of the road, Pilate permits Jesus a proper Jewish burial. No doubt, Caiaphas was not happy about this, but then Pilate had willingly done Caiaphas' dirty work. Why should Pilate care, at this point, what the high priest thinks?

Questions

1) In Mark's Gospel, Jesus is silent on trial before Pilate. Why do you think he did not defend himself?
2) Mark tells us that Simon of Cyrene, innocent bystander, was enlisted to help Jesus carry his cross. His sons, Alexander and Rufus, who were known to Mark's audience were apparently converts to Christianity which suggests their father became a follower of Jesus before them. What about Simon's experience of that day may have attracted him to Jesus?
3) Jesus died for our sins. What does that mean to you?

Chapter 16:1-8

When a parent is walking with a small child, it is impossible to be in a hurry. I remember when our twin sons were about four years old, we were on vacation visiting a park that had an old locomotive and a couple of classic passenger cars sitting on a stretch of track. We spent some time walking around examining train. My wife and daughters had seen enough and walked back to the van. When it was time to go, I summoned the boys and began to leave. Our son Jason, said to me, "Wait for me, Dad! I'm just little."

At the beginning of this narrative commentary, I mentioned that in Mark's Gospel, Jesus is always in a hurry and the disciples have a difficult time keeping up with him in his travels and in understanding his ministry. Jesus may have been crucified, but his followers are about to discover that he is still on the move.

After the Sabbath the women make their way to Jesus' tomb to lovingly finish their obligations toward their Lord. In haste, they could not complete the anointing of Jesus' body before burial. Now that the Sabbath is over, they make their way toward the tomb, after sunrise to do just that.

Their main concern is who will assist them in removing the massive stone that has sealed Jesus' body in its burial cave. The male disciples remain in hiding, either nowhere to be found, or they simply refuse to put themselves at risk by venturing out into the light of day.

To their shock the women discover that the stone, for some unknown reason has been moved. The entrance to Jesus' grave is open. Creating a sense of fear, they encounter a "young man" (an angel?) dressed in white. They are not prepared to meet the living in a place reserved only for the dead.

They then receive the bewildering and unbelievably incredible news. Jesus is no longer in the grave because he is no longer among the dead. He has risen. The "young man" then gives the women a message to his disciples and Peter. Why is Peter singled out separately from the rest? Could it be that because of his denial Peter is, for the moment, out of the band of men who had followed Jesus? Could it more likely be that in mentioning him by name, the "young man" hopes to comfort Peter in the knowledge that his Lord still wants something to do with him, even though he had denied publicly he wanted anything to do with the Lord?

"He is going ahead of you into Galilee. There you will see him, just as he told you." That is the message to the disciples. "He is going out ahead of you." The disciples could not keep up with Jesus in life, and now he has gone out ahead of them into new life. Not even death could slow Jesus down. The Lion of the Tribe of Judah cannot be tamed. Instead, Jesus has tamed the Principalities and Powers. Jesus has entered into the jaws of death itself and pulled its teeth. As he entered into death and has now emerged out the other side into new life, Jesus remains on the move. All the disciples can do is follow him doing their best to keep up. All they can do is obey the command of the "young man"... Go and tell.

Questions

1) Why do you think the "young man" singled Peter out in his words to the women at the tomb?
2) Why would the risen Jesus go immediately to Galilee? Why didn't he stay in Jerusalem?
3) In what ways can we be obedient to the words "Go and tell?"

Chapter 16:9-20

Have you missed the end of a good movie? How would it feel to read an engaging whodunit novel only to discover that the last chapter was missing? We naturally like stories with endings. We dislike TV cliffhangers at the end of one season only to have to wait several months for the rest of the story to be told. How unsatisfying!

Mark 16:8 leaves us with a cliffhanger. The "young man" who is undoubtedly an angel tells the women that Jesus has been raised and he is in Galilee where the disciples need to join him. The women are told to go and tell, but Mark tells us that "they said nothing to anyone, for they were afraid." Wait! What happened next? Did they obey the angel's words and tell the disciples? Did they keep silent forever? Did the disciples meet Jesus in Galilee?

Those of us who know the Jesus story and have three other Gospels to read are well-versed in the answers to those questions; but we must remember that when the Gospels were written, many first-generation Christians were only familiar with one Gospel, two if they were highly fortunate. So, a Christian living in first century Rome, hearing Mark read for the first time have a cliffhanger on their hands when it ends at 16:8. That can't be the end of the story. We want to know more.

Some scholars who have studied Mark thoroughly believe that the writer intended to end his gospel at verse 8; but most, however, including myself believe that there was more and that Mark's ending was lost very early on. The book form with pages as we know it today was invented approximately 100 years after Mark wrote his Gospel. The scroll was the usual way of writing something substantial. The problem with scrolls is that the ends could be easily torn away from the roll if one was not careful. We actually have ancient scrolls with the beginning or ending (and sometimes both) missing. So, it is likely the case that Mark's ending was lost, perhaps even torn away from the original before it reached Mark's audience in Rome. We can't know for sure, but since the Gospel ends as a cliffhanger, it appears to be a reasonable conclusion.

It didn't take too long before people who found this ending unsatisfying decided to write their own and tack it on the end of the story. There is a shorter ending that reads:

> And all that had been commanded them they told briefly to those around Peter. And afterwards Jesus himself sent out through them, from east to west, the sacred and imperishable proclamation of eternal salvation.

I must say that I don't find that ending sufficient. It may tie up some things, but I want more.

Someone composed a longer ending that is contained in most Bibles.

> [9] Now after he rose early on the first day of the week, he appeared first to Mary Magdalene, from whom he had cast out seven demons. [10] She went out and told those who had been with him, while they were mourning and weeping. [11] But when they heard that he was alive and had been seen by her, they would not believe it.
>
> [12] After this he appeared in another form to two of them, as they were walking into the country. [13] And they went back and told the rest, but they did not believe them.
>
> [14] Later he appeared to the eleven themselves as they were sitting at the table; and he upbraided them for their

lack of faith and stubbornness, because they had not believed those who saw him after he had risen. [15] And he said to them, 'Go into all the world and proclaim the good news to the whole creation. [16] The one who believes and is baptized will be saved; but the one who does not believe will be condemned. [17] And these signs will accompany those who believe: by using my name they will cast out demons; they will speak in new tongues; [18] they will pick up snakes in their hands, and if they drink any deadly thing, it will not hurt them; they will lay their hands on the sick, and they will recover.'

[19] So then the Lord Jesus, after he had spoken to them, was taken up into heaven and sat down at the right hand of God. [20] And they went out and proclaimed the good news everywhere, while the Lord worked with them and confirmed the message by the signs that accompanied it.

We know this longer ending of Mark, as it is called cannot be Mark's ending. First, the language is too different from the rest of the Gospel. Second, the ending reports episodes that took place according to Christian tradition later than Mark wrote. Third, it reads like a summary which we do not find in the endings of Matthew, Luke, or John So, while Mark didn't write it, we still have it in our Bibles and translators throughout history have included it, albeit with a note about its lack of originality.

So why is it important to spend some time on this as we conclude our reflections on Mark? It is important because the resurrection of Jesus and his appearances to his disciples and other believers were a central part of the proclamation of the Good News from the beginning. The Gospels not only tell us that the tomb was empty, but that people witnessed an alive Jesus. That is what made the Gospel Good News. This was so central that someone centuries ago knew that Mark's story of Jesus couldn't have ended at 16:8. There had to be more. So, to complete the necessary and crucial ending of the Jesus story, someone attempted to resolved the cliffhanger.

We are Christians two thousand years later only because the tomb is empty and Jesus has been raised bodily. No bodily raised Jesus, no Christianity. If Jesus remained dead, he would be a footnote in history at best—just one more first century Jew crucified by the Romans. His death would have been one more tragedy among others.

The fact that we have singled out his death as uniquely significant can only be on account of the story continuing after his death. So, some unknown believer finished Mark as best as she or he could in order to give the story of Jesus its significance. It is the resurrection of Jesus that makes Mark's story worth the telling.

Two thousand years later, we continue to preach, sing, write, and live the Good News. We too continue to write the story of the resurrected Jesus just as that anonymous contributor did so many centuries ago; only we do so in our lives each day as we seek to be faithful to the new life Jesus has given us.

The ending of Mark's Gospel is not as much of an end as a beginning; and the story is still being told.

Questions

1) Did Mark end his Gospel at 16:8? Why or why not?
2) Is it important for Christianity to have an alive Jesus? Isn't just knowing his tomb was empty sufficient?
3) The Romans crucified thousands of people in the first century. Their memories are lost to history except for Jesus. What is it that has made Jesus significant over the others? The resurrection? His teaching? His memory? Something else?

www.ingramcontent.com/pod-product-compliance
Lightning Source LLC
LaVergne TN
LVHW030635080426
835508LV00023B/3373